TAROT SPREADS

Easy to Follow Layouts for Tarot Readers of All Levels

(A Made Easy Guide for Beginners to Learn Psychic Tarot Reading)

Christopher Kelly

Published by Sharon Lohan

© **Christopher Kelly**

All Rights Reserved

Tarot Spreads: Easy to Follow Layouts for Tarot Readers of All Levels (A Made Easy Guide for Beginners to Learn Psychic Tarot Reading)

ISBN 978-1-990334-68-9

All rights reserved. No part of this guide may be reproduced in any form without permission in writing from the publisher except in the case of brief quotations embodied in critical articles or reviews.

Legal & Disclaimer

The information contained in this book is not designed to replace or take the place of any form of medicine or professional medical advice. The information in this book has been provided for educational and entertainment purposes only.

The information contained in this book has been compiled from sources deemed reliable, and it is accurate to the best of the Author's knowledge; however, the Author cannot guarantee its accuracy and validity and cannot be held liable for any errors or omissions. Changes are periodically made to this book. You must consult your doctor or get professional medical advice before using any of the suggested remedies, techniques, or information in this book.

Upon using the information contained in this book, you agree to hold harmless the Author from and against any damages, costs, and expenses, including any legal fees potentially resulting from the application of any of the information provided by this guide. This disclaimer applies to any damages or injury caused by the use and application, whether directly or indirectly, of any advice or information presented, whether for breach of contract, tort, negligence, personal injury, criminal intent, or under any other cause of action.

You agree to accept all risks of using the information presented inside this book. You need to consult a professional medical practitioner in order to ensure you are both able and healthy enough to participate in this program.

Table of Contents

INTRODUCTION 1

CHAPTER 1: INTRODUCTION TO TAROT CARDS 3

CHAPTER 2: MAJOR ARCANA TAROT CARDS: MEANING AND INTERPRETATION 9

CHAPTER 3: THE POWER AND MEANING OF NUMEROLOGY AND NUMBERS 35

CHAPTER 4: THE ESOTERICISM OF NUMBERS 64

CHAPTER 5: TAROT: KNOWING WHAT IT IS 71

CHAPTER 6: BASIC TAROT CARD MEANINGS 86

CHAPTER 7: CUPS 103

CHAPTER 8: TAROT SPREADS 113

CHAPTER 9: HOW TO GET INFORMATION FROM THE TAROT CARDS FIRST HAND 124

CHAPTER 10: MAKE YOUR OWN TAROT CARD DECK 132

CHAPTER 11: STEP-BY-STEP GUIDE FOR THE MOST IMPORTANT READINGS 140

CHAPTER 12: CUPS 148

CONCLUSION 151

Introduction

Ask yourself this "how much do I really know about tarot cards?" You would be shocked at how misunderstood this simple deck is. It's really not about the pictures on the cards or the "powers" they possess. Our goal is to shed light on the mysteries which reserved for tarot cards. Not only that, but you will clearly learn more after going through each and every chapter.

You won't believe how much misconceptions, beliefs and mystery revolve around the simple tarot cards. Just when you thought that tarot cards were only for creepy fortune telling women in dark little tents, waiting to tell you how unlucky you are at this point.

Readers can go from being confused by tarot cards, to wanting to have their own tarot deck and learning to read some of their friend's fortune. And if you are one of those readers, you will find all the guides, tips and information you need. But if you think that you won't get any kind of benefit, then we'll stop your train of thought right there. Once you get a grip on how tarot cards work, new knowledge wouldn't be your only benefit. Your analyzing skill will be better, you will be able to look at things with a new perspective, greater attention to detail and much more!

Chapter 1: Introduction To Tarot Cards

Each deck of tarot cards contains 78 cards that feature different illustrations that may be interpreted different ways depending on how the cards are laid and what other cards are laid out.

The earliest known tarot cards date back to the 15th century in Italy. It is believe that tarot started out as a card game and was only played by the upper classes but after the printing press was invented the cards became widely available.

Even though tarot cards started out as a card game, in the 18th century they became linked to the occult as well as mystical activities. This began with a free mason in 1781 who claimed that the cards contained hidden messages and they could be used for the purpose of for seeing future events.

Since then many other groups have claimed that tarot cards have mystical powers as well as the ability to tell of future events.

When many people think about tarot cards they think about the scenes we see in movies. A young girl walks into a dark room with cloth covering the walls and old woman comes out sits in a chair and deals a set of cards.

As the young girls sits nervously shaking the old woman's boney crooked finger points and drops to the death card. This is not how it works ever. Many people who don't understand tarot would automatically assume that this reading would mean the girl was going to die but as you will learn later in this book a death card does not always mean death.

Before we move any further there are a few misconceptions about tarot cards that I think we should clear up first. The first misconception is that only psychics can read tarot cards. This is completely untrue. Anyone who wants to read tarot cards can do so. You don't have to have any special gift or ability. All you need is simply a willingness to learn what the cards mean when laid out in a spread.

The purpose of reading tarot cards is not all about telling your future. Sometimes the tarot cards can tell you what is going to happen but the true purpose of a tarot card reading is to help you understand the outcome of your current situation if you continue on the same path you are on right now. Let's look at it this way, if you have a love interest and you get a reading that says if you continue on this path you are currently on you will push this love interest too far, too fast, therefore completely pushing them away you would know to change the path you are currently on.

Tarot is a way to help put your decisions in check and to ensure you are on the right path in order to obtain the outcome you desire.

There are two different types of tarot readings. The first type is an open reading, this means you are looking for general guidance, it does not focus on a specific issue.

Most of the time you will use a question based reading, which focuses on one specific issue that you are facing in your life.

Both of these types of readings are very powerful but an open reading will give you more information towards your life in general. A question based reading will simply focus on that one question you are looking to be answered which is great as well but many times you can miss out on vital information that is needed in your life.

Often times people will already have the answer to their question before they have a question based tarot reading done this will only cause you to receive the same answer you already have through the reading. It is best even if you already have an answer to keep you mind as open as possible. If you are able to keep your mind open during a reading it is possible for you to receive a different answer to your question than what you believe is correct.

For example you may think that it is best for you to switch jobs because you will make more money and have more time off. If you focus on what you think, that this is a good move for you this will be the answer you will receive, however if you open your mind to the fact that you may be wrong and you want to know what you should do than you may find that this is not the best move for you because it will cause more stress in or life and you will be taking on more than you can handle.

When you are using a question based reading you have to maintain a balance when it comes to the amount of detail in your question. Of course you do want to give enough detail to get the answers you need but you do not want to ask such a detailed question that it only leaves the possibility of one answer.

You also need to make sure the question is asked in a positive manner. For example don't ask why you have not been given a promotion but ask what you can do in order to help you receive a promotion.

In an open reading you do not have as much direction but you can still direct the reading to one specific area in your life such as your career, your relationships or your family but that is as far as you can go in an open reading.

Chapter 2: Major Arcana Tarot Cards: Meaning And Interpretation

There are basically two ways to learn how to read tarot cards. Firstly, you need to study and memorize the common symbols used in the tarot and learn the meanings associated with each of the 22 Major Arcana cards. Secondly, you need to learn the way to tap right into your heart and listen to your intuition. You need to connect with your inner being that links you with the rest of the universe. This is the essential framework of tarot card reading.

There are twenty two Major and fifty six Minor Arcana cards, spread across 4 suits: Cups, Pentacles, Swords and Wands. The Major Arcana cards, also referred to as 'trump cards' create the basis of the entire Tarot deck, whereas the Minor Arcana cards deal with the various aspects of your routine life. You will come across various sorts of decks in the market. You need to choose one that you are able to build a connection with. If you can touch the deck, then touch different decks and hold them. Choose one that gives you a strong feeling inside. If you cannot hold them, then look at the pictures of the decks and select one that intrigues and excites you.

Let us begin this journey with understanding the Major Arcana cards and deciphering the meanings associated with all the 22 cards.

What Are The Major Arcana Cards?

The Major Arcana cards create the main foundation of the tarot deck. It comprises of 22 cards of which 21 cards are numbered and one is unnumbered, which is known as the 'Fool'. All the cards symbolize the path to spirituality, self-awareness, and self-efficacy, and signify the different phases we come across in our life while seeking better understanding of ourselves and our lives. This means that they hold within themselves deep meaningful information and lessons.

They also illustrate the basic structure of the human consciousness and provide lessons that have been passed down from one generation to another. The imagery used in these cards is enriched with wisdom and astuteness from several esoteric traditions and cultures from different religions, such as Hindu, Hebrew, Sufi, Buddhism, and Christianity. The 22 Major Arcana cards are also known as the 'Mandalas' of tarot. Mandalas are elaborate images that have been painted on the canvas. They are used as meditation aids and spiritual study guides by the Tibetans. Hence, it is essential to contemplate on the images on these cards to decipher the message they are trying to give you. For that, you need to deeply connect with your intuitive side and try to explore the message the card is trying to send you. You need to seek your personal meaning of these cards to better understand the message.

Role Of Major Arcana Cards In A Reading

When your Tarot reading consists mainly of the Major Arcana cards, then you will be focusing entirely on the life-altering events that you or your client is experiencing. These events have a longer term influence on your life. They give you substantial lessons that you must devote your attention to if you want to move further in your personal and spiritual quest.

One important thing that you need to take care of when carrying out a tarot card reading is to focus all your attention on it. If you or your client are not attentive, most of the Major Arcana cards in a spread will turn out to be reversed. This is symptomatic to not paying attention to the reading and the life lessons being told by the cards, and you need to return to the message of the previous spread before heading forward. You can carry out a tarot card reading with only these 22 major cards. This will give you insight into your spirituality and your mind.

Meanings Of The 22 Cards

Let us look at the names and the meanings of all the 22 Major Arcana Tarot cards. The card number is written above the picture of each card.

The Fool

If it is upright, it symbolizes new beginnings, spontaneity, free spirit, and innocence. If it is reversed, it represents foolishness, naivety, risk-taking, and recklessness.

The Magician

When upright, it signifies skill, power, action, concentration, and being resourceful. When reversed, it shows poor planning, manipulation and hidden talents.

High Priestess

When it is upright, it signifies mystery, high powers, subconscious mind, and intuition. If it is reversed, it shows hidden agendas and the need to pay attention to your inner voice.

The Empress

If it is upright, it signifies beauty, abundance, nature, femininity, and fertility. However, in the reversed condition, it shows dependency on others and creative block.

The Emperor

In the upright condition, the Emperor means authority, structure, father figure and a solid foundation. If it is reversed, it signifies excessive control, domination, inflexibility and rigidity.

The Hierophant

When upright, this card symbolizes group identification, tradition, your beliefs, conformity, and religion. If reversed, it means challenging and defying the status quo and restriction.

The Lovers

When upright, this card means relationships, love, alignment, union, choices, and values. If reversed, it signifies disharmony, misalignment of the values and imbalance.

The Chariot

If upright, it represents will power, assertion, control, determination, and victory. When reversed, it means aggression, and a lack of direction and control.

The Strength

When in the upright position, this card represents courage, control, patience, strength, and compassion. If reversed, it signifies weakness, lack of self-control and self-doubt.

The Hermit

If upright, the Hermit symbolizes introspection, inner guidance, being alone and soul-searching. When reversed, it represents loneliness, isolation, and withdrawal.

The Wheel of Fortune

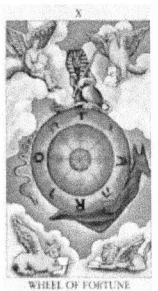

If in an upright position, it signifies life cycles, a turning point in your life, destiny, karma, and good luck. However, if it is reversed, it represents negative external powers, being out of control and bad luck.

The Justice

If upright, it means truth, fairness, cause and effect, and justice. When reversed, it shows lack of responsibility, biasness, and dishonesty.

The Hanged Man

If upright, it represents sacrifice, letting go of things, restriction, and suspension. When reversed, it means delay of things, indecision, and martyrdom.

Death

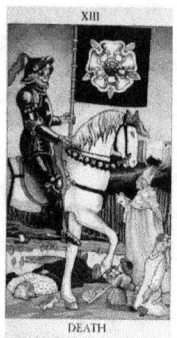

If upright, it symbolizes beginnings and endings, change, transition and transformation. When reversed, it shows the inability to move forward and being resistant to change.

The Temperance

When upright, it shows balance, purpose, intention, patience, and moderation. If reversed, it shows excess, imbalance, and the inability to see things in a long-term way.

The Devil

If upright, it means sexuality, addiction, materialism, and bondage. When reversed, it represents power reclaimed, breaking free, and detachment.

The Tower

If upright, it means upheaval, revelation, sudden change, and disaster. When reversed, it refers to fear of changing and avoiding a disaster.

The Star

When in the upright position, it symbolizes serenity, inspiration, renewal, spirituality, and hope. If it is reversed, it represents despair, lack of trust and faith, and discouragement.

The Moon

If upright, this card signifies insecurity, anxiety, fear, and illusion. When reversed, it shows unhappiness, release of your fears and confusion.

The Sun

If this card is upright, it represents positivity, success, vitality, warmth, and fun. When reversed, it signifies failure and temporary depression.

The Judgment

When upright, it represents inner calling, rebirth, and judgment. If reversed, it symbolizes self-doubt and refusal to examine yourself.

The World

When upright, this card signifies accomplishment, integration, completion of things and travel. If reversed, it represents not getting closure and not being able to complete something.

These are all the 22 Major Arcana cards. You can see that the reversed and upright side of all the cards has several meanings. This is because one card could mean different things to different people. It all depends on the feeling you get when touching and reading a card. Now, let us move on to discussing how you need to spread the cards and interpret their meaning.

Chapter 3: The Power And Meaning Of Numerology And Numbers

Numerology History

Numerology has a long history in places as far evacuated as Egypt, Israel, India and Greece just to give some examples. One rationalist named St. Augustine (354-430 CE) revealed to us that numbers were an all inclusive language from God. He and Pythagoras shared a lot of practically speaking. Both looked to interface numbers to the human personality as well as the interrelationship of all things.

No little errand!

Defenders of Numerology showed up in each period, yet it was around the mid-1800's that we start seeing an increasingly mingled perspective. Much the same as the manner in which the Language of Flowers developed as a quiet correspondence framework between sweethearts, you may discover individuals talking over tea and treats about the discovering genuine romance by utilizing the numbers from their name or birth date. The key numbers for these divinatory endeavors were 1-10, yet there were additionally ace numbers – 11, 22 and 33 (ones that show up in the I Ching, the Tarot, Runes and the Kabbalah).

What is Numerology

From the time we figure out how to talk, numbers become some portion of our day by day reality, throbbing out of sight of life. You have birth date, a standardized savings number, a house number, shoe sizes and cap estimations. The rundown continues forever.

The all-inescapability of digits alone gives us a feeling of their significance ordinarily as well as profoundly as well. Antiquated soothsayers and present day Lightworkers both sense explicit vibrations in numbers, a sort of arithmetical language that keys into different images, signs, signs and examples of the Universe itself.

So continue murmuring!

The standard behind Numerology is that everything in this world has a sort of enthusiastic unique mark – including you! Since the beginning thinkers, masters and aides have grouped these fingerprints with the goal that we can start deliberately grasping the designs that give us signs to the significance of life and our job as otherworldly explorers.

With numbers explicitly, the idea is that the hour of your introduction to the world makes certain conceivable outcomes and impediments, a structure of character. When you know the highly contrasting blueprints, you can even now shading outside them, yet the lines are the beginning stage for upgrading everything in your life including professions and connections.

Here, get a few pastels and how about we look somewhat nearer.

A scholarly Numerologist will never disclose to you that your introduction to the world day numbers entirely characterize you (hell, we as a whole quit maturing at 25 right?).

While the vast majority in the Western world utilize the customary Pythagorean way to deal with number imagery and importance, there are different strategies that don't pursue Pythagoras' at all (in the event that they even ever known about the person).

So we need to take into account some careful squirm room in displaying these seals and the convictions about the manner in which they sway our lives.

How does Numerology work?

So where do you start?

The rudiments of Numerology aren't excessively unpredictable.

Each letter in your conceived an offspring name has a number to which it relates.

By including these numbers in various manners (your complete name, just vowels, just consonants or the numbers in your full birth date) you end up with a profile of qualities.

A portion of the imagery challenges you, a few bolsters and encourages – yet ALL of it relies upon how you apply the data.

A few people have ventured to such an extreme as to lawfully change their names to modify the vibrations in their Numerological build. Should you think about this, recollect the well-known axiom about being cautious what you wish for. To make such a sensational change it's not as basic as simply evolving an "I" to an "E" (aside from after C). You have to (a) recognize what you need and (b) prepare to work for it.

Except if something emotional occurs in your world that would bolster a numerological change, the grass may not be greener with another name by any stretch of the imagination.

Before we go further with our assessment you may be intrigued to realize that Numerology has been utilized in some amazing areas. A few intermediaries use it in anticipating the financial exchange. Others utilize Biblical numerology with an end goal to verify flourishing. The craftsman Prince utilized four digits in naming his collections and even in the manner in which he estimated visit tickets.

Are Numerology Numbers Male or Female?

By their very develop, numbers speak to arrange. One of the sets of life is sex – to be specific male and female. It's idea that odd numbers are manly and even numbers have ladylike attributes.

Brain, you there's some obscuring here so think about this as an extremely broad perception and one that skims just the outside of the data Numerology gives.

Numerology 1

In Numerology the single digit 1 communicates freedom, independence and bent. Individuals with the Life Path Number of 1 are a power of nature – solid in their center, fearless and once in a while somewhat insubordinate. Profoundly, this number speaks to the intensity of Creation itself. As a character number 1s are people who can't remain uninvolved of life for even a minute. 1 consistently drives the accuse of explicit objectives at the top of the priority list. There is nothing without reason for a 1.

In contemplating articulation numbers 1 consistently seems sure. There is no accommodation in Life Path Number 1, nor any equivocalness for individuals who have the character number 1. Like this single digit itself, 1 is straight advance and cement in its reality see. Pragmatics rule over the unrealistic without fail, as does equity and unwaveringness. The Life Path Number 1 can giggle at himself and life, and utilizations that method for dealing with stress regarding their desires for self as well as other people.

Numerology 1:

Number 1's Life Path, Compatibility, and Destiny Meanings

Om, the primary breath of the universe. I Am, the name of God. In the profound criticalness of numbers, these are the establishments for the numerology implications of the perfect Number 1.

As the above all else numbers, 1's imagery is that of the Initiating Force, the Monad. Number 1 is the keynote to joining mankind with one another, Spirit Guides, the Gods and different domains.

Numerology 1 Table of Contents

Life Path

Character

Fate and Expression

Deepest longing and Soul's Calling

Similarity

Vocation Path

Supernatural Associations

Come back to all Numerology Meanings

Life Path Number 1

In the event that your Life Path Number is 1 you most likely shine a different light on being an obsessive worker and Type A character. Your internal enthusiasm pushes you to the cutting edge, always moving toward some objective that to others appears to be inaccessible. You can accomplish really surprising things with your life inasmuch as you recollect that you are a piece of a more noteworthy picture (something 1's occasionally miss).

Most 1's hold themselves to absurd models making them self-basic. They may likewise extend that equivalent grandiose standard on others, not every one of whom can deal with the weight.

At the point when your Life Path Number is 1, the words lethargic and late have no spot in your jargon, nor does reliance and shamefulness.

Some of the time the 1 is the "my way or the roadway" individual (a characteristic of which to be watchful). Indeed, even with such a solid character, 1 individuals are staggeringly creative and can get any task off to a fine start by uniting others. As issues emerge they use "new eyes" for discovering historic, yet down to business arrangements. In any case once that child's out the entryway, let others take care of the subtleties as you may wind up exhausted and searching for that next extraordinary endeavor.

Numerology Personality of Number 1

Character Traits: Original, Individual, Master Creator, Leader, Pioneer, Dominance, The Beginning

1 brings forth all different numbers, and that gives it a touch of well-earned vainglory. 1 individuals can make ponders when they put their brain to it. They disregard obstacles as effectively as forgetting about a light cleaning of day off.

As a rule, it is hasty to hinder 1. Like a bull in a field, you're probably going to get run over. On the off chance that you take a gander at a picture of 1 you can see its pride. You'll know a 1 individual by a head held high, commonly at the front of the pack. At the point when you need to show dreams and objectives, you need 1 on your side for unflinching assurance that conquers the chances.

Notwithstanding, that being stated, Jungian brain research places 1 as an image of solidarity. Like the well-known adage there is no "I in T-E-A-M" when individuals cooperate as one, and have 1 people among them, the progressions that outcome shock.

In the significance of numbers, 1 is the main figure that is neither male nor female. In numerology similarity, when 1 sets with an odd number the outcome is even (female); when hitched with a significantly number the entirety is odd (male). That makes an amazing association for 1 individuals with both Yin and Yang energies working couple. It's no big surprise they make progress toward change and amazing quality with forcefulness.

Regardless, as the tune says, One is a forlorn number. The drive behind this spirit is solid to the point that it might prompt partition. That separation enables the 1 soul to concentrate on their needs and needs, which is consistently at the front line of a 1's psyche. That exceptionally same fixation, in any case, is actually why 1 is an image of administration, enthusiasm and appearance.

1 is most appropriate to a home in which they can handle on-going difficulties that divert them and give imaginative outlets (like a fixer-upper). Such endeavors additionally allow 1's to be in the highlight and hotshot their endeavors.

Regarding leisure activities, 1 searches out challenge, frequently physical. Some that come promptly to mind incorporate boxing, fencing, hand to hand fighting and football.

Number 1 As an Expression or Destiny Number

A Destiny Number of 1 can speak to a first manifestation, or another cycle in your profound improvement. Doubtlessly you'll hunger for autonomy and positions of authority. This implies you'll need to act, now and again excessively quickly. A 1 individual intermittently needs others around them to state "everything in their time" or "there is currently and NOT presently". The 1 individual dislike the guidance yet they do require it.

The enthusiasm for circumstance and serious desire now and again drives individuals with the Destiny Number 1 to bounce from occupation to employment or relationship to relationship. You are continually needing to widen skylines. Simply recall that you can regularly do that without making those jumps. Simply take your circumstance to the following intelligent level.

Out and about of life 1 individuals regularly discover cash effectively and appreciate utilizing it similarly as easily. They will in general travel among little gatherings of exceptionally gifted individuals who can promote their present strategic. It's uncommon that people with this Destiny Number search out profound ways of life. That doesn't mean they're without an otherworldly side yet 1 inclines toward solid idea and activity.

Number 1 As a Heart's Desire or Soul Number

Opportunity implies a lot to you on the off chance that you have a Soul Number of 1. It's one reason we regularly observe 1s in the political field or in the military. In either case, you're in no situation to take orders – you need to be the one in direction. Sadly that obstinacy implies that the 1 thinks that its difficult to connect for help in the midst of hardship. They are likewise not generally the most agreeable of people, shrugging off power when placed in a subservient position.

The sun administers the Soul Number 1, which means these individuals need to sparkle similarly as splendidly. They have a great deal of fire that converts into imaginative contemplations. Such thoughts plan rapidly, and the 1 sticks with them like paste for shelter or bane.

On the off chance that you walk this world with the Soul Number 1 abstain from being excessively reproachful of others, hasty and oppressive. Such practices definitely undermine the 1's prosperity.

Numerology Compatibility of Number 1

On the home front 1 is maybe the most troublesome accomplice. They're regional, regularly requesting and now and then exceptionally basic. 3 and 5 make the best life number accomplices for one. Three is carefree and can disregard 1's not kidding nature, and 5 has an incredible feeling of experience, which means they wouldn't fret joining the party on your next endeavor.

Numerology Number 1 and Career Path

In the event that your Career Number is 1 you may get yourself a solitary fowl, assembling an independently employed profession. This job satisfies you. There's nobody to reply to however yourself.

Different employments fit to a vocation number 1 incorporate military authority, business heads, law requirement, enterprising interests or legislative issues.

Anything having to do with administration satisfies 1's requirement for staunch autonomy and control. Strangely enough the 1 additionally cherishes innovation – the more current the better, so you may discover them on the front line of progressions in that field.

Mystical Associations

Mending Crystals: Angelite, Apache Tears, Aquamarine, Bronzite, Moss Agate, Seraphinite, Sunstone, Smoky Quartz

Celestial: Mars (1) and Mercury (Tarot, The Magician)

Zodiac: Leo and its decision planet, The Sun

Number 1 in the Tarot:

In Tarot Card Meanings and imagery the Number 1 is related with The Magician card in the Major Arcana.

The great Rider Waite Tarot Deck portrayal of this enchanted mage symbolizes the 'as above, so underneath' statute in that he has one hand lifted up toward paradise and one directing descending to the earth.

The Magician predicts achievement in work and in adoration. At the point when a Number 1 keeps their mindfulness open, they have an increased capacity to see mystical chances and can have incredible thriving.

A mover and shaker, The Magician realizes where it counts they can change the world and genuinely have any kind of effect. Having The Magician vibrating with the vitality of the Number 1 implies that they can be incredible facilitators for tense fresh starts that about appear, well, supernatural!

Numerology 2

Numerologists depict the single digit Two as a definitive representative and peacemaker. With this character number, people show tolerance, supporting and delicate to other's needs and emotions. As an articulation number 2 is a definitive ladylike vitality, a delicate mammoth loaded up with class and acumen offsetting the Masculinity of 1. Try not to botch this delicacy as shortcoming. The Life Path Number 2 endures desire about everything life tosses at her.

In the Middle Ages an individual with Life Path Number 2 would be the priceless, shrewd and faithful certain behind the King. She works "behind the blind" where it's anything but difficult to see reality of human practices. Subsequently, those with character number 2 can encourage results without anybody truly realizing she's played her hand. In this long lasting play 2 serenely sits tight for the perfect time and opportunity. Regardless, 2 is an articulation number that murmurs of beauty, refinement, fizz and artfulness that everybody appreciates.

Numerology 3

In the progression of single digit numbers, 3 is the quantity of craftsmen. Those with character number 3 are peppy, astute, gifted and have a young vitality that motivates even the most indifferent people. In any case even with such ability, articulation number 3 needs some direction on the most ideal approaches to apply such moxy, appeal and inclination. A ton of society normally incline toward those with a Life Path Number 3, and not those individuals are gainful.

This number speaks to a ton of good qualities, yet these blessings require discipline. Three involves two numbers together – 1 and 2, so it blends manly and ladylike attributes. Three can be solid and glad, while additionally indicating enthusiastic profundity through their specialty. As an articulation number 3 frequently resists the chances and appears to be very fortunate. A really developed and stirred three gets some distance from instability toward self completion. Now, 3 has incredible intelligence and internal harmony that is so uncommon.

Numerology 4

Among single digit numbers 4 is the most grounded and rational Life Path Number. These are the working drones of Numerology. A character number 3 outlines profound dedication. They are ungainly on the grounds that 4 sees life in solid terms. Number 4 speaks to approach down to minutia. As an articulation number, 4 takes a stab at flawlessness and can be effective in the military in light of their characteristic order.

The 4 character may astonish individuals with showcases of vacant diversion. Four has solid manly hints confirm by a feeling of obligation, morals and diligence. 4 loathes an excess of consideration. The Life Path Number 4 frequently applies to compulsive workers. They pride themselves on subtleties, regularly to the point of missing significant issues on life's peripherals. Regardless this Life Path Number prompts being an excellent supplier and father who may connect as a coach to those with an energy for his field of skill

Numerology 5

In the progression of single numbers, Numerology recognizes five as a fireball. Those with the character number 5 have vitality furthermore, love experience and love a touch of hazard throughout everyday life. As a Life Path Number, 5 discusses somebody with "road" smarts, a sharp personality and a devilish comical inclination. Try not to try and consider enclosing somebody with the articulation number 5 – autonomy is engraved in their spirit. Indeed, even with that eager nature, once in a relationship 5 represents loyalty as a matter of course.

In the work-a-day world, number 5 speaks to on-going change. This individual isn't one to hold a deep rooted vocation. Reiteration demonstrates tedious. Individuals on 5's life way don't generally "get themselves" until the age of 30 when something clicks. Steady employments for individuals with the character number 5 incorporate travel guides, airline stewards or different vocations offering assortment. Regardless of the setting 5 is enchanting, eccentric, mixed and a touch of a weirdo — however individuals throughout her life appreciate those characteristics.

Numerology 6

While 5 was caught up with moving, the single digit 6 was settling down. Numerology proposes 6 is the "mothering" number. As a Life Path Number 6 resounds with dependable, thoughtful ways to deal with life. The language of affection for those with the character number 6 is unquestionably administration. These are healers, overseers and advisors, continually caring for others out of luck. In any gathering setting 6 turns into the nonliteral paste that shields things from self-destructing.

The alert with articulation number 6 is over-doing it. 6 can turn into a meddler. On the other hand 6 disregards their very own needs, regularly at incredible expense physically or inwardly. The number 6 speaks to a profound, tolerating requirement for agreement. 6 recoils from battles and dramatization, finding both offensive. 6 will, notwithstanding, step in when she sees treachery or risk especially in the individuals who can't secure themselves. 6 does well in vocations where they can satisfy the need to help without others exploiting their generosity. Indeed, even in the most noticeably terrible of times life number 6 stays effortless and mindful.

Numerology 7

On the off chance that the single-digit character number 7 had a mantra it would be "look for and you will discover." 7 has an unquenchable interest joined with instinct and diagnostic capacity. There is nothing really easy to those strolling the existence way 7. In Numerology the number 7 speaks to a definitive truth – shallow the truth is only that – superficial and loaded up with figments. That makes 7 socially unbalanced. It's difficult to embed thoughts regarding BIG age-old inquiries at noon discussions.

Those with character number 7 lack the capacity to deal with fakes and trite discussion. They incline toward settings where rationale, approach and certainties make the preparation for activity. 7 battles throughout their life way since they appear to be a smarty pants. This individual can reveal to you odd sound-chomps of information until your gaze goes out into the distance. 7 as an articulation number longs for isolation where they can think obviously. 7 once in a while contemplates profound astuteness, yet with regards to unremarkable issues they've cornered the market.

Numerology 8

Numerology uncovers the Life Path Number 8 as one of parity. Among life and demise, thought and activity, separation and ownership – there is a center ground 8 endeavors to reach. 8 as an articulation number brings regular achievement produced by sensible objectives. 8 underlines an individual's profession and accounts. Among single digits 8 estimates individuals superior to most, which surely helps in business.

Individuals brought into the world with the Life Path Number 8 face difficulties of correspondence. They should live their reality or endure the results of overlooking their own capacity. 8's increase extraordinary riches and free it more than once in their life, yet prosper in any case. Among the single digit numbers 8 comprehends the significance of the material world just as the profound one. Hence, 8 is liberal with their funds regularly utilizing that cash for compassionate causes. They admission well in positions like gathering pledges and riches the board. Extremely all employments where they are a power make sense of turn emphatically.

Numerology 9

The remainder of the single digit numbers, Numerology discloses to us that 9 sees the 10,000 foot view. The expression "think all inclusive" is key to 9s outlook. As a character number 9 outlines complexity, collaboration, innovativeness, certainty and liberality. 9 knows their job on the planet, and applies that through careful activity. The existence way for 9 is loaded up with a wealth of empathy that never falters.

As an articulation umber, 9 reflects ladylike feelings. Love, supporting, giving — 9s possess a great deal of these properties. The vision of mankind in 9s the truth is one where all things interface; everything matter. 9 won't withstand any type of torment, and puts vitality toward goals. This sort of activity is normal of life way 9, looking for no credit or reward other than observing life improved for other people. In the process 9 here and there conceals damages and fears tucked conveniently behind endeavors for the following reason. The closest companion to a 9 is one who challenges those dividers and makes receptiveness.

Numerology 11

In Numerology 11 is viewed as a Master Number. On the off chance that you think about the energies of an actual existence way 1, multiplied you start to get 11. Those with character number 11 are profoundly instinctive and dynamic. Consistently 11 discovers approaches to move themselves to higher aptitudes rationally, physically and profoundly. The number 11 speaks to a raised mindfulness that shows in profoundly precise clairvoyant abilities including mending and prediction. Light Workers disclose to us that articulation number 11 is that of an old soul with incredible intelligence.

Individuals on 11's life way are on a crucial. Their vision is wide and hopeful. The objectives of character number 11 are now and again excessively grandiose; they require establishments and persistence. With those set up, the vibrations in and around 11s life move relentlessly higher. These are the light-bearers and harmony creators. In accomplishing these aspirations and to look after sympathy, 11 must stay open and helpless. This excessive touchiness makes articulation number 11 one that prevails in vocations that require close perception, being in nature or any occupation that feels freeing.

Numerology 22

Numerology paints the Master Number 22 as a definitive designer enthusiastically. Individuals with the existence way of 22 can take a little sparkle of expectation and transform it into a splendid sparkling reality. Like 11, 22 sets numbers together – to be specific 2 and 2. This gives 22 four times the intensity of Master Number 11 and it packs a vortex also having extreme culpability connected. One may consider Master Number 22 as a prototype articulation number that produces amicability and energizes on-going fellowship with the Divine.

At an opportune time, those with character number 22 profit by controlling stray contemplations, being that they can show thoughts in all actuality. Light Workers accept that individuals brought into the world with Master Number Eleven likely could be climbed educators who pick coming back to Earth to make ready for human illumination. That is a colossal assignment, and one in which life way 22 advantages from strong loved ones. For professions articulation number 22 suggests achievement in logical investigations, look into and any field with components of plan.

Chapter 4: The Esotericism Of Numbers

The people of old had an origination of numbers which is nearly lost in modern times. The possibility of Unity in the entirety of its signs prompted numbers are considered as the declaration of total laws. This prompted the adoration communicated for the 3 or on the other hand for the 4 all through artifact, which feeling is so vast to our mathematicians. It is anyway apparent that if the people of yore had not realized how to function some other issues than those that we currently use, nothing could have driven them to the thoughts which we discover current in the Hindu, Egyptian furthermore, Greek Universities.1

What at that point are these activities that our intellectuals do not know? They are of two sorts: theosophical decrease and theosophical expansion. These activities are theosophical in light of the fact that they cause the fundamental laws of nature to enter all through the world; they can't be incorporated into the study of wonders, for they tower above it, taking off into the statures of unadulterated learnedness.

They, accordingly, framed the premise of the mystery and oral guidance trusted to a couple of picked men, under the point of Esotericism.

1. Theosophical Reduction Theosophical decrease comprises in diminishing upset the numbers framed of two or a few figures to the number of a solitary figure, and this is finished by including the figures which create the number, until just one remains. This activity compares to that which is currently called the confirmation by 9.

2. Theosophical Addition Theosophical expansion comprises in finding out the theosophical estimation of a number, by including numerically trouble the figures from solidarity to itself comprehensively. Hence, in figure 4, in theosophical expansion, approaches afflict the figures from 1 to 4 comprehensively, included in other words, 1-1-2 + 3+ 4=10.

The figure 7 equivalents 1 +2+3+4+5+6+7 = 28 = 2 + 8 = 10. Theosophical decrease and expansion are the two activities which are essential to know whether we would comprehend the insider facts of antiquity. 1 Give us now a chance to apply these standards to every one of the numbers, that we may find the law which coordinates their movement. Theosophical decrease gives us that distress numbers, whatever they might be, are reducible in themselves to the nine first since they are altogether brought down to quantities of a solitary figure.

However, this thought isn't adequate, and theosophical expansion will currently outfit us with another light. Through it, Ave locates that 1, 4, 7, 10 are equivalent to 1. The aftereffects of this thought are: (1) That trouble the numbers, in their advancement, imitate the 4 first; (2) That the remainder of these 4 first, figure 4, speaks to the solidarity at an alternate octave.

We see that in every three numbers the arrangement returns to the solidarity unexpectedly, while it comes back to it dynamically in the two halfway numbers. Give us now a chance to rehash that the information on the laws of numbers and the investigation of them, made as we have here demonstrated, will give the way to afflict mysterious science. We can summarize the first articulations in the following end: that afflict numbers might be decreased, in the last examination, to the arrangement of the 4 first, in this way orchestrated.

Be that as it may, our insight into the numerical study of the people of old doesn't end here. That science additionally ascribed significance to each number. Since we have decreased the arrangement of trouble the numbers to the 4 first, it will do the trick for us to know the important credited to these 4 first. The Unity speaks to the Creative standard of numbers, since the others exude in this way; it is the pre-prominent dynamic standard.

Be that as it may, the Unity alone can't create anything aside from by contradicting itself to itself, in this way. From this returns duality, the standard of restriction spoke to by two, the pre-prominent uninvolved rule. From the association of the Unity and Duality continues the third standard, which joins the two contrary energies in one normal lack of bias, $1 + 2 = 3$. There us an overwhelming fix standard. Be that as it may, these three standards decrease themselves into the fourth, which only speaks to another usual meaning of the Unity as a functioning standard.

RELATIVITY BETWEEN THE DEVILISH WORLDS

WHAT ARE ADDITIONAL, NUMBERS?

This succession of numbers 1, 2, 3 and 4, speaking to the dynamic, the aloof, the fix and a second dynamic standard, relates in all focuses with the arrangement of the letters of the Devilish Name.

With the goal that the last may-be in this manner composed, Yod-He-Vau second He = Yod, and so on, which shows analogically that

1 speaks to Yod

2 — He

3 — Vau

4 — the second He

We can demonstrate reality of these analogies by the personality of the activity of the number 4, which turns into solidarity (4=10 = 1), and of the subsequent He, which speaks to the Yod of the accompanying grouping. We would now be able to comprehend why Pythagoras, started in Egypt into the secrets of the sacred word Yod-he-vau-he, supplanted this word in his elusive lessons by the grouping of the 4 first numbers or tetrarchy. This succession of numbers is, in all focuses, indistinguishable with the succession of the letters of the Sacred Name, and the tetrarchy's of Pythagoras, 1, 2, 3, 4, rises to furthermore, totally speaks to the word Yod-he-vau-he.

Chapter 5: Tarot: Knowing What It Is

Despite the many advancements in technology and science that we have seen especially in recent years, many people still believe that "mysticism" or unknown elements have an influence on the events that happened or will happen in their lives. This is why certain practices that were used in order to gain an insight of the past and the future (called divination) continue to exist today. One method of divination that is still sought by many people today is tarot card reading. But what exactly is tarot?

This chapter will explore what tarot cards are and why it is a prominent method in divination.

What is tarot?

The tarot (also called as trionfi, tarrochi, or tarrock) is a set composed of 78 playing cards. The tarot originated in Europe, specifically France and Italy, and was first used during the 15th century to play French Tarot and Italian Tarrochini. Tarot cards are known for having illustrations in order to represent the value expressed in them. For example, the card "Two of Swords" depicts a person holding two swords, while the "Three of Swords" is represented by three swords piercing a heart.

Its involvement in divination and occult

While the tarot was primarily made for playing, during the 18th century, mystics and occultists started using the same set of cards for divination and as a map of an individual's spiritual and mental pathways. Members of the occult believe that the illustrations shown by each card will reveal something about the person who drew or chose the card.

The use of tarot in divination first started in 1540. Based on the book "The Oracles of Francesco Marcolini da Forli", the cards were used for simple divination. This is because unlike today, the cards are yet to be associated with meanings; rather, they were only used for selecting a random oracle. However, manuscripts written in 1735 and 1750 ("The Square of Sevens" and "Pratesi Cartomancer", respectively) provided meanings for each of the cards. Additionally, a system on how cards should be laid out so that proper meanings can be attributed to each card was also provided.

Tarot Card Varieties

The tarot, although known in several parts of Europe at the time that it became popular, was seen in different varieties. There were differences as to the representation of the cards, but all varieties follow the standard – that is, the presence of the suits, the court cards, and the trump cards.

For tarot cards used in the occult and in divination, the format remained the same. However, the occultist Etteilla somehow revised the look of the cards. He believes that tarot cards owed their influence to the Book of Thoth, and it influenced him to design the theme of the cards in ancient

Egypt. He also divided the tarot cards into two parts – the minor and major arcana. This revision eventually led to the creation of other decks such as the Crowley-Harris Thoth and the Rider-Waite-Smith deck. Today, the Rider deck is the mostly-used tarot deck for divination.

Now that you know what the tarot is as well as the short history of how its use in divination came about, it's time to become familiar with the cards themselves.

What's inside a tarot card deck?

It was mentioned earlier that the tarot card deck is composed of 78 cards with different names, suits, and designs. For divination, Etteilla also divided the cards into two parts. But what exactly are the names, suits, designs, and division of this 78-card deck?

Let us first take a look at the parts.

Major Arcana

The first part of a tarot deck is called as the major arcana. It is composed of 22 cards and is arranged depending on the number depicted in each card. Being considered as "trump cards" in a playing card deck, the major arcana can be distinguished because each card has a different illustration. This difference in appearance, translated into divination, simply suggests that cards provide a different meaning as well. Cards in this Arcanum represent significant decisions or events in the individual's life. Their appearance in a tarot card reading also tells of the emotional and spiritual aspects of the person.

Each of these cards, aside from their meanings, is also attributed to a particular planet, element, or zodiac sign.

The following are the numbers and the names of cards included in this Arcanum, along with the attributed planet, element, or zodiac sign for each:

Number	Name	Planet	Zodiac Sign	Element

			(and associated dates)	
0 or 22	The Fool	Uranus		Air
1	The Magician	Mercury		Air
2	The High Priestess	Moon		Water
3	The Empress	Venus		Earth
4	The Emperor		Aries (March 21 to April 20)	Fire
5	The Hierophant		Taurus (April 21 to May 21)	Earth

6	The Lovers		Gemini (May 22 to June 21)	Air
7	The Chariot		Cancer (June 22 to July 23)	Water
8	Strength		Leo (July 24 to August 23)	Air
9	The Hermit		Virgo (August 24 to September 23)	Earth
10	The Wheel of Fortune	Jupiter		Fire

11	Justice		Libra (September 24 to October 23)	Fire
12	The Hanged Man	Neptune		Water
13	Death		Scorpio (October 24 to November 22)	Water
14	Temperance		Sagittarius (November 23 to December 21)	Fire
15	The		Capricor	Earth

	Devil		n (December 22 to January 20)	
16	The Tower	Mars		Fire
17	The Star		Aquarius (January 21 to February 19)	Air
18	The Moon		Pisces (February 20 to March 20)	Water
19	The Sun	Sun		Fire
20	Judgment	Pluto		Fire

| 21 | The World | Saturn | | Earth |

The major arcana can also be called as "The Fool's Journey". This is because the order of the cards represents the journey that individuals undertake – from their earliest awareness (being once "a fool", as represented by card number 0) up until fulfillment (The World). The cards also tell people of the qualities that must be incorporated if they want to fully realize their physical, emotional, and spiritual potential.

By looking at the table above, it can be seen that some cards are associated with a particular zodiac sign. This implies that if a card with an associated sign is found in a reading, the dates associated with the signs are signified. For example, if The Lovers (which is associated with the zodiac sign Gemini) is revealed in the spread, it could signify an event between May 22 and June 21.

The Major Arcana is further divided into two groups. The mid-point is The Wheel of Fortune, marking the two halves of a person's life. Further discussion of the Major Arcana will be provided in the succeeding sections.

Minor Arcana

The second part of the tarot deck is the Minor Arcana. This part usually tells something about the ordinary and everyday aspects of a person's life. It is composed of 56 cards, and has four suits. The suits are as follows (along with other names in which the suit is known):

Wands (can also be called as batons or rods)

Pentacles (can also be called as discs or coins)

Cups

Swords

Each suit of the Minor Arcana is numbered from one (or ace) to ten. This shares similarities with the cards being used today. Each suit also has four court cards, namely: King, Queen, Knight, and Page. The court cards are distinguished from one another by addressing each through the suit where they belong.

Just like the Major Arcana cards, each suit in the Minor Arcana is associated with an element and zodiac signs, shown below:

Suit	Element	Zodiac Sign
Wands	Fire	Aries, Leo, Sagittarius
Pentacles	Earth	Taurus, Virgo, Capricorn
Cups	Water	Cancer, Scorpio, Pisces
Swords	Air	Gemini, Libra, Aquarius

The presence of a specific suit in a reading tells something about a certain area of a person's life, and will be discussed in detail another chapter.

Positive and negative meanings of cards

Every card in the tarot deck (regardless of which Arcanum it belongs) can be associated with a positive and negative meaning. The meanings provided to the clients, though, depend on the card's placement in the spread. For some card readers, they provide the negative meaning if the card is in reverse position (that is, when the card is flipped, it is not in an upright position).

Some guidelines before you get started with tarot card reading

Once you have your own tarot card deck, don't get too excited to give another person a reading. Before doing so, it is necessary that you follow these guidelines first:

You will be able to give a more accurate reading for your clients if the cards are properly handled. Proper storage of your tarot cards will protect it from disturbing energies, which can greatly affect the outcomes that your cards will reveal. To avoid this from happening, your cards should be wrapped in a black cloth. If possible, use a silk cloth. Afterwards, place it in a box.

Don't allow others to use your deck, as it is believed that the connection between the cards and its owner is what enables the cards to provide a more accurate reading to the client.

Spend time meditating while practicing your card reading skills using your deck. This "interaction" somehow strengthens the connection between you and your deck, and this allows for a more accurate interpretation of the cards chosen by your client.

Start familiarizing yourself with the cards once you have your own deck. Look at the cards and write whatever word or phrase that comes into your mind. Have your own journal so that you can write down your personal meaning for each card. Make sure that you're able to think of a meaning for all the cards; if there are cards that gave you a hard time, put them aside first and get back to them later.

Being familiar with the cards and giving each one's meaning through your own words is an important part in tarot card reading. There are only general meanings for each card; its interpretation, though, depends on the one who gives the reading. It is only by doing the last guideline that you're able to further develop your skill in tarot card reading.

Chapter 6: Basic Tarot Card Meanings

The Tarot deck has a great deal of meaning to it and every deck will have a slightly different take on the meaning. Make sure when you purchase a deck you fully read and understand the deck itself. The more familiar you are with your deck the better understanding you will have of it. For now in this chapter we will cover the basic meanings of the cards that most commonly appear in a tarot deck.

The Major Arcana

The fool

This card means many things including: immaturity, sincerity, natural man, free spirit. It stands for one who knows without needing to be prodded or guided their will and has no worries. The fool stands for someone who is a dreamer, someone who is careless, a person who has little interest in practical matters and someone who likes to travel. The fool reversed means some kind of failure, folly, madness or some sort of hindered travel.

The magician

This card stands for A creative spirit, mastery of art, flexibility, autonomy, cunning, perfection of craft and it can also stand for a new beginning in ones life. The magician is a person who knows how to get the goals that he has set for himself and knows exactly where he is going in things. The reversed magician stands for someone who is a trickster, deceitful someone who is full of indecision, weak of will and is inept.

The High Priestess

This is a person with influence that is hidden, this card means silence, patience and someone who is slow but firm in what they are doing. They will always carefully ponder a decision that needs to be made, give advice, and it also stands for a mild form of psychic ability. This card is a full manifestation of the feminine side of spirituality. When reversed this card means someone who is being deceptive, holding a secret, lazy. It can stand for delays, intolerance, doubt and moodiness.

The Empress

This card stands for someone who has understanding, beauty, charm and kindness. It also stands for success, pleasure and a nurturing nature. The reversed means someone who is vain and frivolous. It can mean disdain, carelessness and no care for financial security.

The Emperor

This is a card of power and stability. This card can mean being in full control of yourself or a situation and someone who is a leader, a dominate. When you see this reversed it stands for a loss of control and emotional issues. It can stand for stubbornness and an ill temper as well.

The Hierophant

This card stands for wisdom and endurance. It also stands for a person with persistence , patience and who offers good advice. It can mean that you are okay with getting help from those who rank above you and that you know your inner-self. When you see this card reversed it means that you tend to be to concerned with the morality and issues of others. That you can be illogical, superstitious and unable to behave coherently.

The Lovers

A card that means union, marriage, love and marriage. It is also a card that suggests attraction and a certain balance and openness as well as harmony. If this card is shown in the reverse it means dangerous temptation, a wrong choice and a broken relationship with infidelity.

The Chariot

A card of Triumph and Will this card means one who is in control of themselves and who is able to overcome opposition. It is someone who can control their own destiny and it can also mean good news. When shown in the reverse this card means illness and the possibility of a dangerous and violent accident.

Justice

This card stands for a conformity of moral high ground, whether in action or attitude. It stands for the power to remain balanced and handle the responsibilities of life. It stands for someone who knows that sometimes things must be sacrificed for the greater good, it can also stand for law, trials and marriage. When shows in the reversed it can mean someone who is a fanatic, insecure and imbalanced. It can also mean that a harsh judgment is coming.

The Hermit

A card of patience and wisdom, silence and that of a spiritual person. It can mean someone who has become divinely inspired or someone who has found an inner solitude. It is a card that can mean someone is in search of something spiritual. Reversed this card stands for stubbornness, viciousness and immaturity.

It also means someone who is overly shy and who may have enemies they don't know about.

The Wheel of Fortune

This card stands for change and evolution for good fortune and fate with a pinch of success thrown in. When you see this card in reverse however it will mean delays and setbacks.

Strength

When you see this car it means for a regulation of passions, power and energy. It means there is great love and that spirit will take over in matters. It can mean action and courage along with power and success. When you see this card in reverse it can be ruin in your life, stubbornness and an abuse of power.

The hanged man

This card means a certain kind of inner fortitude and self imposed limitations along with wisdom. It can mean that you are going to be redeeming yourself soon through a form of sacrifice or loss. It can also mean that a choice is coming which you must think about carefully. When seen in the reverse the hanged man means arrogance and failure. It can also mean wasted effort.

Death

Contrary to popular belief this card does not just mean death it can also mean rebirth and evolution. It also stands for transformation and change. When seen in reverse this card means a broken marriage or someone who is terminally ill. It can also mean true and vile death.

Temperance

This card stands for someone who is careful when they make choices and who is patient and does everything in moderation. It can also stand for self control, the ability to adapt, and exercise self restraint. This card also stands for a good marriage and the ability to work well with others and show good management skills. When you see this card in reverse it means disorder, conflict and a bad set of combinations. It can also mean arguments and the breaking of a marriage.

The Devil

Also known as Fate this card means blind impulse, seduction, seductive power, temptation, obsession and sexual deviance. It can also mean that earthly powers are turning you inside out. When you see this card in reverse if can mean weakness and blindness, disorder and a harmful fate.

The Tower

This card stands for sudden changes that happen with no choice. It means an escape from bondage or prison and a collapse of something around you. It can also mean bankruptcy or a sudden death. When in reverse this card can mean a complete confusion of facts and it can also mean you gain freedom but it will come at a cost that may not make it worth it. Lastly it stands for oppression.

The Star

This card stands for hope, clarity and insight. It can also mean you will get help that you did not expect and great love can be given or received. It also means good health. When in the reverse however this card means stubbornness, arrogance and a bad judge of character or ideals.

The Moon

This card stands for intuition or for a moment of being on the threshold of making a great change in your life. It can mean your path is not fully clear and it will be difficult to walk. When seen in the reverse this card means Sudden and unknown perils will happen and you have enemies that you do not know about. It also means hysteria or a possible blackmailer in your midst.

The Sun

A card of glory and one that means material happiness. It can also mean a happy marriage or relationship of any kind, success and pleasure. It will also mean you have great energy and through this will achieve success. When seen in reverse this card stands for annoyances and arrogance. It can mean you will have a broken engagement or lose your job sometime in the future.

The Universe

A card that means success will come your way, great rewards are around the corner. It can also mean you will be traveling soon, change your residence or your country of residence. When you find this card in reverse it can mean you are about to come under stress, find hindrances in life and that hard work is ahead.

The Minor Arcana

The suit of Swords

King: A serious card it can mean there is a controlling person in your life, it also means control, focus and intellectual.

Queen: This card stands for intelligence, communications yet a frigid person.

Knight: A fierce fighter who can be aggressive/Fierce, determined, aggressively pursues goals

Page: A person who is mentally not all there and who is immature. This person often acts without mentally conceiving. Mentally unstable or perspicaciously immature, acts without cerebrating.

Ace: A sense of clarity with a new start.

2: Indecision

3: Betrayal

4: Rest meditation, rest, retreat

5: Hostility mind games, hostility

6: Acceptance of help

7: Abandoning a situation

8: Feeling powerless

9: An anxious person

10: Feeling of defeat

Suit of Cups

King: Repression of feelings

Queen: An emotionally nurturing person who is also sensitive

Knight: Romance

Page: A person who is creative and full of artistic skills

Ace: Joy

2: Attraction and compatibility

3: Celebration with friends

4: Boredom

5: Self pity

6: Kindness and sentimentality

7: Indecision

8: Abandonment

9: Indulgence

10: Happiness

Suit of Wands

King: A mature and passionate person

Queen: Confidence

Knight : A risk taker

Page: Fresh inspiration

Ace: Fresh start

2 : Contemplation

3: Receiving benefits

4: Safety

5:Small struggles

6: Success

7: A person who feels on guard

8: Speed

9: Preparation for the worst

10: Oppression

Suit of Pentacles

King: Financial security

Queen: A balanced and healthy person

Knight: A cautious person

Page: A student

Ace: A person with set goals for life

2: Balance

3: One who enjoys their work

4: Hoarding

5: Small time money issues

6: A Charitable person

7: Patience

8: A hard worker

9: Luxury

10: Financial success

Now that you know the basic meaning of all the tarot cards you can begin to feel more comfortable with your deck. Spend time with them, memorize the meanings to each of your specific decks. Once you have become comfortable with the meanings it will be time to do some of your first readings.

RWS Tarot - A Brief Introduction

The Rider Waite Smith Tarot deck is probably the most popular and well known of all tarot decks that are available today. The name comes from William RIDER & son-the original editor, Arthur

Edward WAITE-the academic and mystic who commissioned the creation of this game, and Pamela Colman SMITH-the talented but often neglected artist, who drew pictures from the Rider-Waite Tarot game (as it is often called). Waite and Smith were both members of the Order of Golden Dawn, the famous but fleeting occult group of the 19th century.

RWS tarot card game was released in 1909 and was the first widely available game with illustrated minor arcane cards. Fifty-six tiny arcane cards, also known as "pecks," today had a wealth of symbolism displayed in the pictures, as well as twenty-two major mysterious cards. Until then, less mysterious cards on the tarot deck showed only four cups, or six chopsticks or eight swords. RWS tarot cards with illustrated "pips," as well as evocative images of the main Arcana, finally revolutionize the world of tarot cards. When Waite designed his tarot package, he maintained a basic sequence of cards, even as he changed card numbering and fairness in the main Arcanes. There is debate about who actually designed the minor Arcane cards. It was said that Waite designed and gave Smith full instructions or just told her your thoughts and gave free rein to their artistic talents to create images. Each card carries a monogram of Pamela Colman Smith, usually in one of the lower corners.

The original print of the albums was tragically destroyed in the London bombing, and the release ended. In 1971, US Games Inc. he began publishing a protected fax version of the game.

These days, many bridges follow the basic pattern of the RWS tarot deck. There are RW versions that were re-colored, but kept on designs of this original line. Versions that have been redesigned usually have the same basic numbers and parameters on maps with similar symbolism. Game type RWS is generally recommended for beginners, because the basic visual scenes may be more easily associated with keywords, to make it easier to memorize and understand the meaning of each card. However, there are also many experienced readers whose favorite reading platform is an RWS or variant. Most books for beginners and beginners use illustrations of the RWS bridge for learning purposes.

One thing is certain, if Arthur Edward Waite and Pamela Colman Smith didn't have to work together to create a tarot deck-RWS tarot would be very different from what we are accustomed to today.

Chapter 7: Cups

The Cups depict emotion and spirituality. They dig deeper into your emotions and help you identify your feelings on your relationships.

Ace of cups- the ace of cups is a good card as it signifies love and compassion for others. It also marks an overwhelming emotion that a person might feel towards others and the kind of intense love that they have for others. It marks the beginning of a new love relationship. This card signifies fertility as well and marks the fertility of a woman. The reversed card signifies an excess of emotions and the person will cry for a long time after a relationship ends. But in reality, the person is much stronger than that and is capable of displaying strong emotions. The person will suffer from emotional ups and downs.

Two of cups- the upright two of cups card signifies love and attraction. It deals with the creation of a new being. This new being can be power and beauty combined owing to the coming together of two people. It signifies the instant attraction that one has towards another person. The reversed card signifies a struggle and the lack of trust between two individuals. It will also indicate a break up between two people and the lack of harmony between two people. If a break up does not occur then it means that the people are not in love and are only lusting for each other.

Three of cups- the three of cups card signifies friendship and creativity. It promotes creativity and a sense of community. The card showcases three people gathering in a circle and raising a toast. The upright card means that the person is helpful and loves helping others. It also signifies creativity and the positive growth of a person. The reversed card signifies that the person is going to have heartbreak and the relationship is about to end. It might also indicate the person's isolation from others. It means that the person has lost contact with their close friends and this might be because of a work commitment or a fight.

Four of cups- the four of cups card signifies reevaluation and the interest in meditation. It also indicates a struggle that you are having in trying to fix an old problem. It also signifies that somebody has proposed a good thing to you but you are not taking it seriously, nor do you have any interest in it. The card showcases a man sitting under a tree and looking down while a cloud is handing him a scroll. This means that the boy is disinterested in turning to the world and prefers to look down. The reversed card signifies that a positive change is about to come through. You will have the chance to open up about your emotions to someone and not hold any of it inside you. You will finally break away from your current state and help yourself.

Five of cups- the five of cups is generally regarded as being a bad card as it can signify loss and sadness. There will be a lot of regret and are unable to let go of your past. It means that the person has lost a lot in life but there is still hope and the person can get back whatever has been lost. The card showcases a person in a black cape who has turned away and has his head bent. The reversed card can signify the person's acceptance of their situation and the strength to move on. It also signifies that the person will now take risks in order to break away from a safe environment.

Six of cups- the upright six of cups card signifies the rushing back of memories and nostalgia. The person starts to remember their childhood memories and will look to the good times to derive inspiration. This card can also signify that you are soon going to be in an environment that you had when you were a child. It will mean that there is still a child inside of you and you are humble, creative and spontaneous. The reversed six of cups card can signify you not being able to move on from your past. You are holding on to something that is connected to your past and are not ready to move past it.

Seven of cups- the seven of cups card signifies that the person is full of fantasies and has vivid illusions. Their imagination is quite diverse and is capable of dreaming up beautiful and awe-inspiring dreams. The person will mostly be dreaming things that do not really exist and are just figments of imagination. This card also signifies that the person's fondest wishes will come true. The reversed seven of cups card signifies that the person is hiding something from themselves and are not accepting the fact their illusions are only imaginary. They will forge ahead with a dream even if it is impossible to achieve.

Eight of cups-the upright eight of cups card signifies that the person is a state of withdrawal and in a position to stay away from everything that the person has achieved. The person is disappointed and has no faith left in love and the ways of this world. The reversed eight of cups card signifies hopelessness and a lack of determination. It also indicates that the person is not confident in doing anything and has given up on many things in life including hope. If things start to get tough then you prefer to run away from the situation instead of staying still and facing it. This can get a bit overwhelming at times and you will be disappointed in yourself.

Nine of cups- the upright nine of cups card signifies that the person is happy and satisfied and has all of his wishes fulfilled. This can be regarded as being a state of personal development and indicates that you have attained success in all fields of life including health, life, wealth and relationships and are completely satisfied. The card showcases a person sitting on a throne with a satisfied expression and there are nine golden cups placed on top of the throne. The reversed nine of cups card signifies the person is dissatisfied and their wishes are not materializing which is upsetting the person. It indicates ill fortune and a sense of gloom and dissatisfaction. The person might indulge in smoking, drinking and do drugs, which will mark their downfall. It will also indicate that the person has no regard for others and is only bothered about themselves.

Ten of cups-the upright ten of cups card signifies that the person is headed towards marriage and is going to be happy very soon. There will be an alignment in their relationships and will soon have good fortune doling into your life. You will have a very good family life where there will be a lot of love and respect for each other. You will basically have a loving and fulfilling family life. The reversed ten of cups card signifies that there is an emotional block in your relationships and they are not functioning properly. It can indicate that you are not valuing your family and are taking them for granted. You are after material things and have decided to forgo your family's happiness.

Page of cups- the upright page of cups card signifies that you are on the verge of starting something creative and are determined to see it through. This can include dance, drama and other forms of fine arts. You will discover a new side of you and be able to live out your childhood fantasies. In fact, you will be united with your inner child and start to look at life innocently. You will find no bad moments and have a lot of love and compassion for others around you. The reversed page of cups card signifies that you are immature and don't love yourself enough. You are prone to childishness and can throw a tantrum every now and then, which makes it tough for others to take you seriously. If this card pairs with the devil card it means that the person is prone to drug addiction and other such bad habits.

Knight of cups-the upright knight of cups card signifies that the person is up to undertake adventures and is keen on exploring passions and underlying ambitions. So it is best to tap into all of your inner ambitions and explore all your pet hobbies. The reversed knight of cups card indicates that the knight is making you jealous of someone or something. He will make you do illogical things that you would not otherwise be doing. The person might have to stop and observe their behavior to understand what is happening to them. It also indicates that a beloved relationship is changing its face. What was once nice and interesting is now sadly different. This is making the person restless and he or she is not able to lead a normal life.

Queen of cups- the upright queen of cups signifies that the person is calm and mature and is aware of the ways of the world. They are intuitive and compassionate towards others. They are emotionally stable and make for loving wives and caring mothers. If this card shows up then you need to focus on caring for others and understanding their need for love and attention. The reversed queen of cups card signifies that you have lost touch with your true feelings and are now slightly brash. In fact, you have been treading on this path for a while and might have reached a point of no return. But there is hope and with time, you can get acquainted with your emotional side again and start looking at the world differently.

King of cups-the upright king of cups card signifies that the person is in good control and is emotionally stable. It is safe to say that the king of cups has the highest control over his emotions and feelings and does not lose stability easily. They will be extremely calm even when faced with adversity. They will be collected and take the best possible decisions that will suit everybody. The reversed king of cups card signifies that person is quite emotional and allows emotions to guide him. It will also signify that the person is immensely confused emotionally and is not sure who their true lover is. This can lead the person to trust anyone and everyone and end up having a lot of heartbreaks.

Chapter 8: Tarot Spreads

What are Tarot spreads

There are many spreads you can use, and most tarot books include some samples. There is no need to use much spread but pick some so you can quickly get the hang of it. Be comfortable with your pick and develop an understanding of which situations you should use the best.

When reading, be guided by your intuition to determine which spread is best, and you don't need to ask why. You may likewise design your spread like "Finding a New Job Spread. One card may be for the kind of work that will suit you best then another for your current job. Another card for what you need to do to get the job you want most. You may add more to these. Write the meaning and position of each card in the spread so you will have a clear view of how it works.

The most challenging thing that people have faced is to pick the correct spread that they could use for their reading. They are unable to identify the spread that works best for them. There are quite a few spreads that are available and you will not be able to identify the best spread for you right in the beginning.

Most Tarot card layouts or spreads range from one card from a deck to an entire deck! Each of these spreads has its own unique characteristic that provides the spread with divination powers. There are quite a few Tarot spreads that have become standardized, but there are quite a few readers out there who have been able to develop their own layouts, as they deemed necessary.

These layouts are based on the adjustments that the reader wants to make to the layout he is most accustomed to.

Five Card Spread

The Five Card Spread helps the people know what course of action to take next. As it says on the name, you take five cards and place one in the middle. Next, you put one card on each side of the middle card, it kind of looks like a cross now.

Card 1 (in the middle): the general theme of your reading.

Card 2 (left side): represent some past issues that still affect the present.

Card 3: (right side): shows the future.

Card 4: (bottom card): the main reason behind the question, it can even help give more information about number 2.

Card 5: (top card): all the potential within the situation.

Subconscious impulses are shown in card number 4 or even something that's stopping you from achieving what you want. While card number 5 shows some possible result if they do take the course of action.

It's better if you focus on the aspect of your potential decision while choosing your cards.

The Eclipse Spread

Another spread that helps answer your questions is the Eclipse Spread, which is made up of seven cards. The first card should be placed first on your left side, continue placing the next card next to the first one. The rightmost side should have the seventh card, it should also look like a wide V where the first and last card are aligned. Also, the middle or fourth card should be the lowest one.

Card 1: Past events that still influenced the current situation.

Card 2: All the influences that surround you as of the moment.

Card 3: Future influences that may weigh in the situation.

Card 4: What you need to do right now.

Card 5: All the outside forces or influences that have effect.

Card 6: All your hopes and fears.

Card 7: This represents the possible result of the situation.

The most crucial card in this situation may be the fourth one, the answer to your problem or question.

The Pyramid Spread

In recent years, there has been an increased interest in anything Egyptian, and as a result it is no surprise to see a spread called the pyramid.

Key

CARD 1 = Main circumstances prevailing

CARD 2 = Alternatives worth considering

CARD 3 = Alternatives worth considering

CARD 4, 5 and 6 = Events which led to present circumstances and the forces at work behind the scenes

CARD 7, 8, 9, and 10 = Best way in which we can either resolve the problems or deal with them

This is another easy spread to use, and is particularly successful in helping with specific issues or difficulties which may be present. Having shuffled the pack, any 10 cards can be used in the order shown above.

The 21-Card Spread

Another spread which can be used is the 21-card spread. This again can help with future developments, but requires skill and a great deal of practice to use appropriately, bearing in mind the number of cards used and the categories into which these falls. It is probably a spread to aim for when you have practiced the others several times first.

Key

Column 1 = The person concerned and their present state (1, 8 and 15)

Column 2 = The situation around the person (2, 9 and 16)

Column 3 = The hopes and fears of the person (3, 10 and 17)

Column 4 = Expectations (4, 11, and 18)

Column 5 = The unexpected (5, 12, and 19)

Column 6 = The near future (6, 13 and 20)

Column 7 = The long-term future. (7, 14 and 21)

Many people use this spread when dealing with problems of career and home, although obviously it can be used for any area of difficulty. It is always worth bearing in mind what we have learned about month cards in this spread, and indeed others, as it might then be possible to be more specific on the timing of events, especially when dealing with things to come.

The Celtic Cross

This one might be a little difficult and confusing since it has ten cards, but it is actually one of the most common and used card spread. The Celtic Cross is the best spread if you want some of your specific questions answered.

The first step is to create a Five Card Spread on your left side. Next is to take the second card and place it on the middle card of the Five Card Spread.

Take note that when you place it above the middle card, it should be in a horizontal position. Lastly, take your remaining cards and form a vertical line on the right side of the Five Card Spread. The tenth card should be the one on top, the seventh in the bottom.

Card 1 (middle of the Five Card Spread): Represents the present

Card 2 (card placed on top of the middle card): This represents the immediate challenge that you face. A challenge that you need to overcome. But if you have a good card here instead, think hard because it still represents a challenge.

Card 3 (right card in the Five Card Spread): The root of the problem found in the distant past.

Card 4 (bottom of the Five Card Spread): A much more recent past, this also includes some events. This may not be the min root of the problem, but it's fairly connected.

Card 5 (above the Five Card Spread): The best possible outcome, though it still can't compare to card number 10. However, if this card is a negative one, you should cut your losses immediately.

Card 6 (left card in the Five Card Spread): The immediate future which indicates the next few days or weeks.

Card 7 (bottom of the horizontal card): Possible inner feelings that significantly affect and influence the situation.

Card 8 (above card 7): All the possible external influences. This may be people or events that can't be controlled.

Card 9 (above card 8): The hopes and fears regarding the situation or problem. This card can be confusing most of the time. If it gets too confusing, draw another card and evaluate both of them.

Card 10: The outcome, usually a self-explanatory card. Though if it proves to be also confusing, you should draw three more cards for clarification.

Roundabout Spread

The Circle / Cross has two crosses – the smaller one which is in the center consisting of two cards which are enclosed in the bigger cross consisting of six cards. The cards at the top of the cross depict your conscious mind while the cards at the bottom of the cross depict your unconscious.

The cards in the Staff section talk about your life and they usually do not deal with the present. To interpret the meaning of the cards in the Celtic cross spread you have to let yourself be guided by your unconscious. You will be able to understand your future better and also help people understand their future better.

Chapter 9: How To Get Information

From The Tarot Cards First Hand

Now that you have an understanding of what these cards have to offer, you are ready to try and conduct your very own reading. To do so, you will need to follow some basic preparatory steps. The first is to take the deck in your hands, and turn it such that the pictures are on the underside of the deck. Then you need to shuffle the cards well, cutting the deck at least twice as you do so. Once you have shuffled them thoroughly, you are able to start your reading.

To begin with, think of the question that you would like an answer to. Make sure that it is at the very top of your consciousness. Then you need to decide in which formation you will lay your card out so that you can find the answer that you seek. This is known as the tarot card spread. Here are several spreads that you can consider.

The Celtic Cross Spread

If you have had an encounter with someone who has conducted a tarot reading for you, it is likely that they used the Celtic Cross Spread. This is perhaps the most widely used spread that you will find today, especially for people who are using the Rider Waite tarot deck. The reason that this spread is highly popular is because it offers valuable insight on various aspects of one's life, which provides a rich and holistic answer to any question being addressed.

As the cards are being laid out, it is important to focus on the question that you would like answered.

This spread features a total of ten cards. The first card is in the middle of the space where you are carrying out your spread, and the second card will rest on top of the first card. The third card is located directly above the first and second card, while the fourth card is placed directly below these cards. The fifth card is placed on the right of the first and second card, whereas the sixth card is placed on the left.

The seventh, eighth, ninth and tenth cards are positioned in a column to the right of the fifth card. In this column the seventh card is at the bottom, and the eight card above and so on until the tenth card at the top.

Each position that the cards are placed in has a meaning as follows: -

Position 1

This position is indicative of the present state that you are in. It is known as the Significator.

Position 2

This position reveals forces that oppose you or which have an influence over you. It is known as the Crossing.

Position 3

This position looks at where your question actually came from. It is known as the Foundation.

Position 4

This position considers what has occurred in your past in regards to events, and anything that has caused you concern. It is known as the Recent Past.

Position 5

This position looks at that you have placed importance on in the present, as well as what could possibly occur in the future. It is known as the Crown.

Position 6

This position looks at what you can expect to experience on your future path. It is known as the Future.

Position 7

This position addresses the way that you are emotionally, in the present moment. It is known as Emotions.

Position 8

This position looks at who may have an influence over your life, and the way that your relationships with other people are working out. It is known as External Forces.

Position 9

This position addresses what you really hope and what you would like to happen as a result of the question you have asked. It is known as Hopes and Desires.

Position 10

This is the likely result of the question that you have asked. It points at what is possible, and should be related to all the other cards within the reading. It is known as the Outcome.

The Relationship Spread

Many people consult tarot cards for a reading when they are dealing with relationships with others. This is not restricted to romantic relationships, but also includes relationships at work, at home, with friends and family.

This spread allows one to find out more about their relationships, as it offers insight into the needs of all that are involved. To get an answer from this spread, as you are laying out the cards, think about the relationship that you have with a particular person, and then consider the question that you would like to ask. Ask the question and then spread the cards. This is how you should position them.

You will create a column in the middle of your table. This spread will use a total of nine cards. At the bottom of the column you will place the first card, and then above it, the second third and fourth card. Above the fourth card, you will place the sixth card. To the left hand side of this card, you will place the fifth card. To the right hand side, you will place the seventh card, and then the eight card. Above the sixth card, you will position the ninth card.

Each position that the cards are placed in has a meaning as follows: -

Position 1

This card will offer you insight on the way that you view the other person in your relationship.

Position 2

This card will offer you insight on how the person you have the relationship with views you.

Position 3

This card will help you identify the needs that you have within the relationship.

Position 4

This card will then identify the needs of the person you are in the relationship with.

Position 5

This card will help you understand the present position of your relationship.

Position 6

This card lets you know which direction you would like the relationship to take.

Position 7

This card lets you know which direction the person you are in the relationship with would like the relationship to take.

Position 8

This card reveals other things about the relationship that you need to keep in mind.

Position 9

This card reveals the possible outcome to the question that you have asked.

Being able to use these true steps will get you on the right path towards making sense of what the tarot cards can reveal to you when you do a reading. By using them, you will discover how easy it is to conduct your own reading, and to make sense of any situation that you may be facing. You will also get answers that could reveal what is really happening within your present situation, and the possible outcome that you can expect in the future.

Chapter 10: Make Your Own Tarot Card Deck

A Tarot card game is something that many people want to use, but I do not know which formula to choose. The number of tarot games available can be surprising to some. And while you might like a few tarot card games, you may not be able to afford more than one. Instead of wasting time looking at the tarot decks available, it's time to make your own tarot deck exactly to your specifications.

You will need some supplies before making a tarot pack for you. To begin with, you need a thicker quality paper on which you can make drawings of Tarot. If you find a paper with a pattern on one side and an empty area on the other, everything is better. Take this paper and cut it into 78 corresponding squares or rectangles, to your liking. Then collect artistic needs to create drawings on the empty side of the paper. Things like markers and colored pencils are ideal because they do not rub.

If you want to imitate the ideas of a traditional tarot card pack, you will want to look for a real tarot card pack or a card online. This way, you can start with an idea for each card, but you can create your own unique patterns. Look at the examples of tarot as simply inspiration; it does not have pictures that you need to copy. For example, you can make a five-stroke, but the chopsticks can look as you like, and there may be other background images you call.

Finally, to complete the package, you need to create a safe place to stay when it is not in use. You can buy a box or bag that can be used to store your cards, for example. And then you can decorate this box or bag to help you make this room something more personal and special. Some people also choose to laminate their cards to add a layer of protection and stability.

Regardless of your reasons for wanting a tarot, remember that you do not need to spend a lot of money or even adhere to "traditional" models. To see the future, you can start with the cards created by your own hands.

How to Predict the Future Using a Tarot Deck

Is it possible to predict the future? What about the Tarot deck? Yes, it is! Read on, and you'll find out how.

Extract your favorite tarot pack or fortune teller. It is better to stay in a quiet space, but the most important thing is to work with cards. All these are amazing tools that can help create a contemplative atmosphere. It works best with a tarot card or Oracle decks, asking open questions rather than yes/no questions. Some open question tips are listed below. Yes/no question would be how to tear off daisy's petals, "does she love me? Or don't you like me?"I have a raise."

What kind of energy will I have to monitor in July?

My annual exam is scheduled for the last week of March. What areas of improvement will be discussed in my review?

I'm going to propose to my girlfriend. What is the most favorable Week and day to ask her?

My son is starting a new school. What energy do we need to know about his school? Will the change make him succeed?

Tomorrow is Monday, what kind of energy do I meet at work? House? On the highway?

Take your time, formulate, and explore each question. Make sure the question is exactly what you want to know. Vague questions will give you vague and often frustrating answers. An example of a vague question can be: "why can't I find a good job? Instead, you might ask, "What kind of energy do I have to get a better job?"

After formulating and considering your question on the day you wanted education, take the Tarot platform (or Oracle platform). Mix the cards and think about your question. Download the map. Meditate on the map. Note the story that the map tells you or the story that makes you think. It could be Little Red Riding Hood, or Uncle Ted came across a piece of wildflower. History does not matter, neither real nor fictitious. Look at the colors and what they represent for you. Look at the numbers, the time, the symbols you see on the maps. Do not forget about the traditions of Tarot meanings.

During meditation, focus on the map of the symbol, shape, or color that represents the shapes of the map. Let the shape, symbol, color dance in your head until you form the next one. In the calendar, write it or draw it and all other information you received. Do not judge the information that comes. Write down what it is. The image of a ship sinking in the Blood Red Sea may not mean a real wreck. It could be a prediction that the 15th day In January of next year, the company you work for may have a huge drop in the price of their shares and are left in the red financially. Pay attention to everything, regardless of whether it makes sense or not.

To what extent it is necessary to request information in the future. If you want to know about next week or about seven months in the future, it doesn't matter. Tradition says not to ask more than six months in advance, because the energy around the event, the person, etc. can change. However, the same applies to any reading. Two hours later, energy could change for up to two decades in the future.

If you have received forecast-based information, you should consider reconnecting to maps a week or a month before the forecast date. People change their minds, learn new skills, and someone may die, they can become all sorts of things that can affect time. Whether something changes or not, you have a strong answer. If things are completely different, you can find out what new energies will affect that day.

Be vigilant for cards, labels, symbols, colors, etc. that are repeated in each of your predictive data. The more something is repeated, the more news it is.

If you read about other people, pay attention to the repetition in the cards; if you see one or more cards, it repeats again and again, regardless of the person reading. This occurs mainly for four to six months. Attention. If a map of the tower appears at each reading, this could mean another collapse of the bank. If the moon appears, it could mean that we have an emotional turn for the event. In either case, a map or not a map, this repetition means that change is coming. Something is happening socially, politically, or economically.

Start predicting your future, pull up the calendar, or turn on the phone. Extract any tool to maintain a normal life. Using tarot cards or Oracle decks, you can predict the future.

Chapter 11: Step-By-Step Guide For The Most Important Readings

In this chapter, it's time to make the transition from theory to practice. After you have been introduced to the theoretical world of tarot, you now have the basic information for the most common readings: **the personal reading** (a personal reading about and for yourself), **the external reading** (when you are interested in finding out a specific detail about another person), and **the general reading** (when you are not interested in a specific problem and you simply want to receive more information about your general position in the world).

The Personal Reading

This is probably the type of reading that you will be using the most. It can be done both for a specific answer that you want to receive, and for a daily reading – when you want to know what to expect from the following (or the current) day. Thus, you can either perform this reading right before you go to sleep the day before, or when you wake up and prepare for a new day. Of course, you can read for yourself at any daily moment, if a certain situation appears all of a sudden, and you feel the need for a more meaningful insight on how you should proceed.

The most important aspect of the personal reading is that it needs to be, just like the name says, personal. It must be about you and for you. No other person can be implied directly or indirectly. However, you can check, for example, the way in which you should act towards a person close to you, but the center of interest must remain your own person. Another aspect that might be as useful to you, as it is to me, is keeping a diary. By writing down your evolution over a longer period of time, you will be able to observe what cards you selected more often, and see if the elements really describe you, and your life, or if there is any change that you should make.

The External Reading

If the previous type of reading must be centered only on your own person and needs, we also need something to give us certain details about things that are not directly connected to us. These readings can be about people, the general future, a certain event, animals, and even the world in general. The idea is that the final interpretation of the answer depends on how broad the subject of your question is: for problems implying groups, or, for example, the future of our world, the answer will be extremely vague.

This is why you should decide on a specific center of interest, which will be the focus of attention. The question that you will write down, and that you will repeat (aloud or in your mind) while shuffling the cards. Although I emphasized the fact that, for this reading, you must take your person out of the problem of concern, it must be understood that, when interpreting the result, you might discover that certain elements could be attributed to you as well. These situations are especially common when you try to find out something about a person close to you.

The General Reading

Another method that will probably prove helpful in the future is the general reading, or asking your tarot cards to guide your general evolution in the future. We usually need this reading when we are preoccupied or stressed for some reason that is beyond our power to discover. Thus, by doing a general reading, you can find what is causing – maybe on the unconscious level - your distress. But you can also do it with no specific interest in mind. In this case, it should be done only from time to time, and, preferably, before a major event in life (in order to keep it on a different level than your regular, daily readings).

For this, there is no need for a specific question to be narrowed down. This is why you can either skip the third step from the following list, or replace it with a more thoughtful concentration on yourself, and the things that you would like to find out. You can openly state your confidence in the power of the cards, and in your own instinct. Also, you have the possibility to perform multiple general readings if you feel the need to narrow down a bit the area of interest. For example, one time you can think about your love life, then about your health, and so on.

9 Steps that You Need to Follow for Any Successful Reading

1. Put things in order and prepare all the items that you will need for the reading. Before actually beginning the act of reading, you need to take care of everything else that is a potential disturbance. In other words, you need to clear up your mind of anything that might not let you concentrate: feed your pets, give your children an activity to keep them occupied, take care of your urgent daily chores, turn off your phone, and so on. Then, prepare the cards, and go to your special place.

2. Enter the mood. As I already explained in a previous chapter (go back if you need those details again), a certain state of mind is necessary for a successful reading. Try to relax, and think about the problem that currently disturbs you. When you are ready, take a piece of paper and write down the correct formulation of your question.

3. Ask the question. After you have reached the necessary level of concentration, take the cards in your hands and think about your problem. Then, ask the question out loud, as if the person who could provide you the answer were in front of you.

4. Shuffle the cards. While still thinking about the question and the general context of your problem, start shuffling the cards. Do it for as long as you want, and in the way you are most comfortable with.

5. Cut the cards. When you are done shuffling, put the entire deck in front of you. Divide them in three smaller piles starting from a card in the inside that you feel attracted to. Then, put them back together. Remember, the cards need to remain face down.

6. Spread the cards in the shape that you want (The Celtic Cross in our case). Carefully, create the pattern by placing the cards in front of you. This time, the cards need to be set face up.

7. Make your analysis of the cards. Check or try to remember the meanings of each card, and, at the same time, the position in which they are placed. Choose the elements that are most representative for your situation. Be objective and realistic. Write down the key elements, if you think that this will help you with a better interpretation.

8. Connect the results for the general interpretation. Try to see if you can connect the characteristic features of each card, in order to create some kind of story: from past to present, and from the unconscious to conscious, for example. Try to summarize the entire interpretation, as to obtain a one-sentence answer for your question.

9. What's next? After putting the cards in order, it's time to think about the real purpose of the question. How does the answer help you? What can you do to correct your previous mistakes, and respect or put in practice the things that you have just learned about? Before returning to your daily routine, make sure to find a way to put the newly-discovered details in practice.

Chapter 12: Cups

Cups or Chalices are another name for hearts in the original playing deck and they also stand for the element of Water and their cards are about emotions and love.

Ace of Cups - Upright: tender feelings, love, overpowering emotions, and artistry.

Reversed: inhibited or obstructed emotions

Two of Cups - Upright: alliance, appeal, and united love.

Reversed: inequality in a relationship leading to breaking up, and no cooperation between two people.

Three of Cups - Upright: companionship, parties, artistry, and association.

Reversed: prevented artistry, cheating on your love, and too many people around.

Four of Cups - Upright: feelings of reflection, indifference, contemplation and reconsidering. Reversed: someone who is uninterested, has been remote and distant, and feels they have lost a lucky chance.

Five of Cups - Upright: someone who suffered misfortune, feels heartache, letdown, and hopelessness. Reversed: someone who has gone on and shown consent and absolution.

Six of Cups - Upright: someone who is recollecting their childhood, feeling sentimental, and blamelessness. Reversed: someone who isn't practical, too trusting and is stranded in the past.

Seven of Cups - Upright: someone living in a dream world, who daydreams, and has an excessive fantasy world, and has wishful thinking. Reversed: alluring distraction, takes detour strategies, and deception.

Eight of Cups - Upright: letdown, prevention, and desertion. Reversed: despair or walking away without a goal or wandering without direction or purpose

Nine of Cups - Upright: contentment, desires, bliss, and accomplishment. Reversed: unhappy in life, gluttony, and desire for possessions.

Ten of Cups - Upright: marriage, tranquility, and bliss. Reversed: broken marriage or values not lining up together.

Page of Cups - Upright: the start of something artistic, a coincidence in time, and someone who brings good news. Reversed: artistic block, someone who is feeling childish.

Knight of Cups - Upright: someone coming to deliver you from danger, allure, love affair, and intense fantasy. Reversed: someone who is crabby, impractical and envious.

Queen of Cups - Upright: someone who is allowing serenity in their life, feeling safe, and kindness. Reversed: someone who has an unhealthy psychological reliance on another person, afraid and apprehensive.

King of Cups - Upright: someone who is equalized and fair, and has mastery of their emotions and themselves physically. They are also very giving. Reversed: someone who is crabby, explosive and emotionally devious.

Conclusion

You might be a little shock as to how misguided some of your beliefs were. We are glad that you have a better understanding of how tarot cards work now. Now more misguidance, profound beliefs and just a little less mystery involved. But as you have read all the details, wouldn't it be fun to learn how to tell your own fortune? To be able to confidently say that you really know how to use a tarot deck?

We are not saying that you need to be the best in the world, who will have fun in that kind of pressure? Just be happy and devoted to this simple art. After all, what's praise and hard work if you actually hate what you're doing? So go out there, buy your own deck and see how many windows of opportunities and happiness awaits you along the way. Remember, this isn't a simple thing that you can learn overnight, you need to have patience. Don't forget to expect mistakes, that's normal after all, so don't be afraid to commit them and learn your valuable lessons from here on out.

www.ingramcontent.com/pod-product-compliance
Lightning Source LLC
Chambersburg PA
CBHW071451070526
44578CB00001B/304